P9-DFY-778

Living on the Edge
SCUBA DIVING

Shane McFee

press™
New York

Published in 2008 by The Rosen Publishing Group, Inc.
29 East 21st Street, New York, NY 10010

First Edition

Editor: Joanne Randolph
Book Design: Kate Laczynski
Photo Researcher: Jessica Gerweck

Photo Credits: Cover, p. 1 © Stephen Frink/Getty Images, Inc.; p. 4 © www.istockphoto.com/Martin Strmko; p. 6 © Superstock.com; p. 8 © www.istockphoto.com/Dave White; p. 10 © www.istockphoto.com/Carrie Winegarden; p. 12 © www.istockphoto.com/Marco Crisari; p. 14 © Getty Images, Inc.; p. 16 © www.istockphoto.com/Dennis Sabo; p. 18 © www.istockphoto.com/Tammy Peluso; p. 20 © www.istockphoto.com/Miguel Angelo Silva.

Library of Congress Cataloging-in-Publication Data

McFee, Shane.
  Scuba diving / Shane McFee. — 1st ed.
      p. cm. — (Living on the edge)
  Includes index.
  ISBN 978-1-4042-4217-3 (library binding)
  1. Scuba diving—Juvenile literature. I. Title.
  GV838.672.M385 2008
  797.2'3—dc22
                                                  2007034535

Manufactured in the United States of America

CONTENTS

What Is Scuba Diving?

Have you ever held your breath under water? You could not do it for very long, could you? You had to come back to the surface, or top, to breathe.

Have you ever wanted to stay underwater for a long time? Maybe you should try scuba diving. Scuba diving is a fun sport that makes it possible to swim underwater for a long time.

Scuba diving **equipment** allows people to breathe underwater like they would on land. It also allows people to see and to move underwater. Do you want to learn about scuba diving? Keep reading!

Scuba diving opens up a whole new world to divers. Imagine having the chance to swim with beautiful fish like these!

Like a Breath of Fresh Air

Some of the first scuba divers were soldiers in World War II. They wore special machines called rebreathers. Rebreathers allowed them to breathe underwater. A rebreather reuses the air that you breathe out. There is very little wasted air.

The famous ocean **scientist** Jacques-Yves Cousteau helped make the scuba equipment that we still use today. He called his invention the aqualung. It was an important discovery. It allowed divers to breathe underwater for a long time. Cousteau invented the aqualung so he could study **marine** life.

Soldiers with rebreathers could swim underwater without being seen. They were sometimes called frogmen.

SCUBA

SCUBA stands for "self-contained underwater breathing apparatus." In other words, scuba is a **tank** of air that the diver carries on his or her back. A hose connects the tank to the diver's nose and mouth.

It is hard to see underwater. Scuba divers wear special masks that allow them to see clearly underwater. Scuba divers also wear special outfits called wet suits. Being in water too long can cause a person to get too cold. Wet suits keep divers warm. Scuba divers wear fins on their feet instead of shoes. They are shaped like fins of a fish. They help divers swim.

These two divers check their equipment before a dive. You can clearly see their tanks and wet suits.

Scuba School

Does scuba diving sound like fun? It is, as long as you know what you are doing. There are many skills you must learn. The most important skill is breathing with the equipment. You also need to learn how to watch how much air you have left. You do not want to be diving in deep water and run out of air! You can learn these skills by taking classes.

To rent or buy scuba equipment, you need to have a scuba **certification**. There is no set number of hours a diver needs to finish before becoming certified. The diver must master all the skills needed to dive safely, though.

These divers are practicing breathing during their scuba lesson. The teacher makes sure each student can dive safely.

Scuba for Fun

Scuba diving is well liked in warm places where people go for vacation. Many of these places have fish that are beautiful and strange. Scuba diving offers an excellent chance to see these fish up close.

One kind of scuba diving is called wreck diving. Wreck divers **explore** shipwrecks. Shipwrecks are exactly what they sound like. They are the old remains of sunken ships. Wreck diving is a great way to learn about history and old boats. It is also a good way to find old, historical objects. Wreck diving is not always safe, though. Beginning divers should not try it.

This diver explores a shipwreck. Lots of sea plants and animals make their homes in old wrecks.

Scuba on the Job

Not all scuba divers swim for fun. Some people scuba dive for work.

The **military** still uses divers to swim into places without being seen. The military also uses divers to fix holes or other problems in Navy boats.

People in the Coast Guard also train as divers. They often search for and rescue, or save, people lost at sea. Police officers and rescue workers dive to search for people lost in lakes and rivers.

Just like Jacques-Yves Cousteau, many scientists also dive so they can study plants and animals that live underwater.

Here a Coast Guard diver jumps from a helicopter into the ocean. These divers must train for long hours to do their job well.

Underwater Pictures

Have you ever watched a TV show about fish and other animals that live in the ocean? Did you wonder how the filmmakers got a camera under water? Do you wonder who took the underwater pictures in this book?

Some people take underwater pictures when they are on vacation. Others are **professional photographers** who train to be scuba divers.

Taking pictures under water is not like taking pictures anywhere else. It can be very hard. The photographer needs equipment that can work under water. Many photographers train for years to take beautiful underwater pictures.

This underwater photographer is taking a picture of a lionfish. Lionfish are just one kind of beautiful animal that lives in the sea.

Pressure!

Scuba diving is not always as safe as people think. This is not just because of sharks and other animals. The water itself can hurt a diver.

One of the biggest underwater dangers is the **pressure** of the water. Have you ever dived to the bottom of a deep swimming pool? Did you feel the pressure on your ears and nose? This pressure is caused by all the water. That swimming pool was not very deep. Imagine diving over 100 feet (30 m). That is a lot of pressure. Master divers know how to swim in deep water without hurting their ears.

This diver explores sea caves on a dive. Cave diving can be unsafe, and is not for beginners.

The Bends

Sometimes divers come up through the water too quickly. This can really hurt a diver. The water above has less pressure than the water below. This means coming back up does strange things to the water in your body. Coming up too quickly can cause **decompression** sickness. Decompression sickness is also called the bends. The bends forms gas bubbles in your blood. This is very painful and even deadly.

Scuba divers should watch the bubbles that they breathe out. They should never rise faster than their bubbles.

These divers are coming back to the surface after a deep dive. They are taking care not to come up faster than their air bubbles.

Dive In!

Do not let all the dangers of diving scare you. If you know what you are doing, scuba diving is safe and fun. There is no other way to stay underwater for so long and see so many marine plants and animals.

Do you want to learn more about scuba diving? Ask your mother and father to help you **research** it. You can find out more about diving schools on the Web or at the library. Look for scuba diving centers the next time you are on vacation, too.

Does scuba diving sound like the right sport for you? Jump in! The water is fine.

GLOSSARY

certification (ser-tuh-fuh-KAY-shun) Something that shows that you have passed a test.

decompression (dee-kum-PREH-shun) The letting go of pressure, or a force that pushes on something.

equipment (uh-KWIP-mint) All the supplies needed to do something.

explore (ek-SPLOR) To travel over little-known land.

marine (muh-REEN) Having to do with the sea.

military (MIH-luh-ter-ee) Having to do with the part of the government, such as the army or navy, that keeps its citizens safe.

photographers (fuh-TAH-gruh-ferz) People who take pictures.

pressure (PREH-shur) A force that pushes on something.

professional (pruh-FESH-nul) Someone who is paid for what he or she does.

research (REE-serch) To study something carefully to find out more about it.

scientist (SY-un-tist) Someone who studies the world.

tank (TANGK) Something that holds matter, like air or water.

INDEX

A
air, 7, 9, 11
aqualung, 7

C
certification, 11
Coast Guard, 15
Cousteau,
    Jacques-Yves,
    7, 15

D
decompression
    sickness, 21

E
equipment, 5, 7,
    11, 17

P
pressure, 19, 21

S
shipwrecks, 13

T
tank, 9

W
water, 5, 9, 11,
    17, 19, 21–22
World War II, 7

WEB SITES

Due to the changing nature of Internet links, PowerKids Press has developed an online list of Web sites related to the subject of this book. This site is updated regularly. Please use this link to access the list:
www.powerkidslinks.com/edge/scuba/